Bentley C
Bentley Ne

Early Development

Dave Fordham

Fedj-el-Adoum Publishing

Published by Fedj-el-Adoum Publishing,
3 Adelaide Road, Norton, Doncaster, South Yorkshire, DN6 9EW

© Fedj-el-Adoum Publishing & Dave Fordham 2009

ISBN 978-0-9562864-1-3
First Edition 2009

Acknowledgements

The author would like to thank the following for their assistance in compiling this work:

John Fordham & Paul Fox for suggesting improvements to the manuscript; BarnSCAN - *The Barnsdale Local History Group*; Mr Stan Longley; the staff of Doncaster Archives; Helen Wallder and Carol Hill from Doncaster Local Studies Library for allowing access to contemporary newspaper records from *The Doncaster Gazette* and *The Doncaster Chronicle;* the staff of The National Coal Mining Museum for England Library and The University of Birmingham Library for viewing their holdings of *The Colliery Guardian;* Caroline Carr-Whitworth of English Heritage; and the many picture postcard publishers whose work has been used to illustrate this publication, in particular Edgar Leonard Scrivens and James Simonton & Sons. Unless otherwise attributed, all illustrations featured in this publication are from the author's collection.

Cover Illustration

Bentley Colliery around 1914 from a commercial postcard published by Edgar Scrivens. By this time Bentley Colliery was about to enter a sustained period of maximum production. The building work is complete and this includes the ferro-concrete hempstead structure beneath the headgear of No 2 shaft. Coal was raised from the shaft to the upper level of the hempstead structure before being transported to the screens off to the right of the picture.

Bentley Colliery

Towards the end of the 19th Century, Bentley was an agricultural village situated on the Selby Road, 2 miles north of Doncaster, within the parish of Arksey, called after the ancient settlement of Arksey which lay on the eastern side of the Great Northern Railway, the main line from London to Edinburgh. By this time the road from Bentley to Doncaster had been largely bordered by a ribbon development of late Victorian houses and in 1903 Bentley was connected to Doncaster by the Doncaster Corporation's electric tramway.

Bentley High Street, from a postcard by John Crowther-Cox of Rotherham. This view shows High Street looking towards the junction which would later become known as Playfair's Corner where the road forked to either Askern or Arksey. At the time of this photograph in c1905, Bentley village was a rural settlement with a few farms and cottages and the post office on the left.

The local landowner was Sir William Cooke who resided in Wheatley Hall on the other side of the River Don from Bentley. In the 1880s, Sir William Cooke was very confident that coal lay at a depth of around 600 yards beneath his estate despite the fact that the nearest colliery was at Denaby a few miles to the west where the coal seams were nearer the surface. At this time land owners were eager to exploit the new found mineral resources beneath their estates because the income from coal royalties would make a substantial contribution to estate incomes. In 1885 Sir William Cooke entered into negotiations with the Vivian Boring & Exploration Co. Ltd. from Whitehaven. As the name suggests this company was a small engineering concern, under the control of Mr John Vivian, who specialised in drilling boreholes to prove the existence of coal seams beneath the surface. Mr Vivian intended to lease the coal royalty from Sir William Cooke, prove the existence of the Barnsley Coal Seam beneath the Bentley area and then sell on the lease to the mining rights at a profit to an established colliery company. The lease covering a royalty of 4,000 acres included coal seams beneath the estate of Sir William Cooke and also around 1,000 acres of land owned by the Chadwick family of Arksey Hall.

In 1887 Mr Vivian and his team of men made a start at drilling a borehole at a site near Bentley Mill. By 1889 they had reached a depth of 600 yards without encountering the Barnsley Seam. At this time it is reported that the boring tackle fell down the hole and could not be retrieved and the borehole would have to be abandoned. Not perturbed by this Mr Vivian moved to a new site in Daw Wood Plantation and commenced the drilling of a second borehole. In 1893 this second borehole successfully encountered the Barnsley Seam at a depth of 615 yards and proved the existence of a 9 foot thick coal seam. Consequently a formal lease was drawn up between Sir William Cooke and The Vivian Boring & Exploration Co. Ltd. dated from the 1st September 1894. This lease of 4,000 acres included an annual payment to the Wheatley estate which increased from a minimal rent for the first 5 years to £2,000 in Year 6 and every year thereafter, plus a royalty of 3.5d payable on every ton of coal produced.

However, in 1895 Sir William Cooke died and he was succeeded by his son, Sir William Henry Charles Wemyss Cooke, who with death duties to pay and no income from the coal royalty apart from a peppercorn annual rent from Mr Vivian was anxious to move the project forward. Two colliery companies had expressed an interest in developing a pit in the Bentley area. These were Henry Briggs & Co. Ltd. who owned several pits in the Wakefield area and The Clay Cross Colliery Co. Ltd., proprietors of collieries to the south of Chesterfield in Derbyshire. Clay Cross declined to take up the option at Bentley and Henry Briggs after considering the project for a few years finally declined in November 1899. Another approach made to Henry Briggs was also rejected in June 1901. The reason for the rejections by these well established colliery companies was probably due to the projected expense of sinking a colliery to a depth of over 600 yards which at the time would have been one of the deepest in the country.

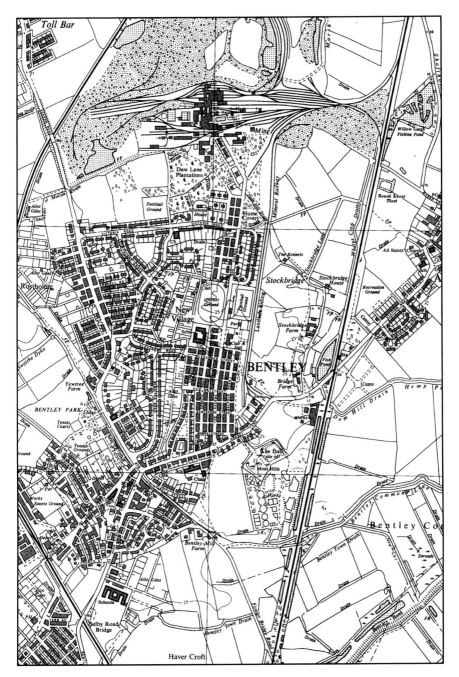

This extract from the 1966 Ordnance Survey 6" to the mile map features some of the areas mentioned in the text. Bentley Colliery is situated to the north of Bentley New Village. Wheatley Hall was located off the map to the south-east on the other side of the River Don. (Crown Copyright reserved).

As a result of this Mr Vivian was left with 615 yards of rock core locked away in his warehouse in Doncaster and with annual lease payments to Sir William Cooke which by now was costing him £2,000 per year. He tried to interest some of the other Yorkshire colliery companies in the idea but with no success. At the start of the 20th Century he moved his men and equipment to undertake the drilling of a borehole at Hampole for the Hickleton Main Colliery Co Ltd. and it looked like the Bentley project had been an expensive waste of time.

However, on the 29th October 1901 a meeting of Barber Walker & Co. was held at their head office at Durban House in Eastwood, Nottinghamshire. This company had been formed in 1787 from the merging of the collieries owned by the Barber family of Lambs Close, Eastwood, and those of the Walker family of Eastwood Hall. Barber Walker & Co. Ltd. owned 5 collieries in the Erewash valley near Nottingham which produced a combined total of 727,989 tons in 1896, and the company had been valued at £350,000 in 1890. However, they were well aware that their coal reserves were rapidly running out and at the 1901 meeting Mr Robert Barber put details of the Bentley project to the Board and it was agreed to make further enquires.

Consequently Mr Thomas Barber, the chairman of Barber Walker & Co., journeyed north to Doncaster to meet Mr Vivian and see the rock samples from the Bentley boreholes. Mr Vivian, by now probably getting a little desperate, wanted £10,000 to gain access to his warehouse containing the rock cores. Presumably the £10,000 requested by Mr Vivian included taking the Bentley lease off his hands. This appears to be a somewhat extortionate figure but maybe Barber Walker were equally desperate to replace their declining coal reserves as they paid Mr Vivian £5,000 to see the cores and promised to pay him the balance if they took up the lease. Thomas Barber thus viewed the rock samples in the company of Mr Vivian, who (possibly due to having to pay Mr Vivian £5,000 to see a lump of coal) he later described as "a little fat chap"!

Returning to Nottingham a further meeting of Barber Walker was held on 27th March 1902 where Mr Barber could not contain his joy at what he had seen. He described the coal seam at Bentley as "a heart warming thickness of coal superior to any they had experienced in Nottinghamshire and they should back the main chance". As a result of the depletion of their Nottinghamshire coal reserves they purchased the lease of 4,000 acres from Mr Vivian and decided to go ahead with the development of a large colliery at Bentley capable of producing 1,000,000 tons per year, significantly more than the rest of their collieries combined output.

A site was selected in the centre of the area of land covered by the lease near Daw Wood not far from the site of the borehole and in 1903 Barber Walker appointed Mr Green, formerly General Manager of J & J Charlesworth Ltd., owners of several collieries in West Yorkshire. Mr Green was charged with overseeing the sinking operations. He made arrangements with Sir William Cooke to increase the lease from 4,000 to 6,940 acres and constructed two roads, later to become The Avenue & Victoria Road, to access the site. Arrangements were made with the Great Northern Railway to build a short branch line from their main line in order to deliver the machinery required for the sinking.

In 1904 it was reported that work was expected to start immediately with the sinking of two shafts for the new colliery. The new venture was initially referred to as Arksey Colliery. However, it soon became known as Bentley Colliery. Unlike several of the neighbouring Yorkshire collieries, the suffix Main was never applied to Bentley Colliery.

It was expected that the project would cost £500,000 for developing the pit and building the colliery village and would find work for 200-300 men to sink the shafts. When the pit was completed it was expected to employ up to 3,000 men and produce an output of 4,000 tons of coal per day. It was also stated that they expected to experience problems with water which proved to be true. Although the company intended to provide all the machinery and workforce themselves they commissioned the Doncaster mining contractors Messrs Walker & Eaton to undertake the actual sinking work. This concern had just finished the sinking of two shafts for Sherwood Colliery near Mansfield and nearer to Doncaster they had previously sunk the shafts at Manvers Main and Hickleton Main Collieries.

As well as leasing 6,940 acres from Sir William Cooke, including 1,000 acres beneath the estate of the Chadwick's of Arksey Hall, Barber Walker purchased outright the Scawthorpe estate to the west of Bentley which comprised Scawthorpe Hall, Scawthorpe Grange and three lodges on the Great North Road, together with around 1,000 acres of farmland. This gave Barber Walker a coalfield of nearly 8,000 acres at Bentley and as well as becoming colliery proprietors they also became farm owners and farmed the Scawthorpe estate. The Company also negotiated with Sir William Cooke for the outright purchase of 75 acres of land near the colliery which would form the site of Bentley New Village, a purpose built community to house the workforce required at the colliery.

*Above: Sir William Cooke lived at Wheatley Hall until he left the area for his Oxfordshire estates in 1924. Wheatley Hall survived as a golf course club house but was finally demolished in the early 1930s when the surrounding land was purchased by Doncaster Corporation and laid out as part of the Wheatley Hall industrial estate. **Below:** Some of the coal extracted at Bentley Colliery was leased from the Chadwick family who lived in the more modest Arksey Hall before they also left the area. Arksey Hall has survived as a home for the elderly. (Postcards by Edgar Scrivens).*

On the 16th March 1905 a small ceremony was held at the Bentley site to mark the cutting of the first sod of the new colliery. Mrs Green, the wife of Mr Green, the site supervisor, performed the honours and gave a short speech where she expressed her good wishes for the success of the enterprise and her hope that the contractors and their men would get through their work without accident or serious interruption. It was proposed to sink one shaft first and when this had been completed the second shaft would be started. It was expected that it would take between 3-5 years to sink the shafts which would be 20 feet in diameter.

However, each visit of Mr Thomas Barber to the Bentley site increased his anxiety about the slow and unsatisfactory progress being made under Mr Green's control since he had been appointed. At a Board meeting of Barber Walker, Thomas Barber expressed his opinion that Mr Green was not competent to carry out the sinking and he was dismissed only a few weeks after his wife had cut the first sod. Mr Green was replaced with Mr John Fryar of Bettisfield Collieries in North Wales, who took up his duties from the 2nd May 1905 and was appointed General Manager later that year.

Although the first sod had been cut in March 1905, work in sinking the shafts had not actually commenced until 9th October of that year when the sinking of the No. 2 or upcast shaft commenced. According to the Daw Wood borehole it was expected that they would have to pass through 50 feet of waterlogged sands and alluvial deposits before they reached solid rock. It was expected that these unconsolidated sediments would cause extreme difficulties to the operations due to their water content as they were described by Mr Fryar as "quicksands".

To overcome this, cast iron tubbing would be lowered into the sand to form a complete circle and the quicksand could then be removed from the centre. On reaching a depth of 50 feet they hoped to encounter the top surface of the bedrock through which sinking the shafts would be considerably easier. Things proceeded to plan until they reached a depth of 50 feet and there was no sign of the top surface of the bedrock as had been expected. A small borehole was drilled in the shaft which showed that the depth of quicksands actually extended 100 feet from the surface. By the end of 1905 water was beginning to flow into the shaft bottom and the iron tubbing lining was beginning to crack and deform due to the pressures of the surrounding quicksand. Mr Fryar was left with no option but to abandon the shaft and start again in the New Year using lessons that had been learned from 1905.

On 3rd March 1906 the sinking of the new upcast No. 2 shaft commenced on a site a small distance from the earlier abandoned shaft. This time the new shaft would be 23 feet in diameter, with a circle of iron piling surrounding an inner circle of iron tubbing encasing a brick lined shaft which would hopefully have the strength to hold back the surrounding quicksands. Work now commenced at a steady pace despite the occasional mishap with the flowing sands and water filling the base of the excavation and requiring the use of large electric pumps capable of removing 8,000 gallons of water per minute. The top of the bedrock was reached at a depth of 100 feet on 6th June 1906. Despite the problems with the quicksand Barber Walker were pleased that they hadn't had to call in continental engineering experts to do the work for them.

Once solid rock had been reached it proved to be a relatively straight forward operation and sinking continued down through the Triassic Bunter Sandstone, Permian Magnesian Limestone and into the Carboniferous Coal Measures. To aid this process the temporary sinking apparatus was replaced with a permanent wooden headgear and brick built engine house and this was used to complete the sinking of the shaft through the solid rock strata. Finally on Saturday 4th April 1908 the shaft struck the Barnsley Coal Seam at a depth of 624 yards and the directors were pleased to announce that the seam was 9 feet 4 inches in thickness.

Earlier, the 22nd September 1906 had marked the start of work on sinking the No. 1 or downcast shaft and using experience gained in sinking the No. 2 shaft the process of sinking proceeded very fortuitously and the Barnsley Seam was located at a depth of 624 yards on October 30th 1908. To celebrate the discovery of coal in both shafts Barber Walker & Co treated the 300 pit sinkers on the site with a dinner served in a large marquee in Arksey Lane. Following this, the mining contractors, Messrs Walker & Eaton and their staff of sinkers, left to undertake a new assignment in sinking the shafts of Thorne Colliery which would also prove to be a challenging piece of engineering.

Simultaneously with the sinking of the shafts, the construction of the surface plant was planned so that it would be in position to raise and treat coal as soon as the Barnsley Seam was reached. Both shafts had been provided with wooden headgears and brick built engine houses that were equipped to raise the coal which was transported to a German built "Luhrig" coal washing and screening plant situated above the extensive sidings that the Great Northern Railway had constructed. A small power station provided the steam power to drive the winding engines and drive the air ventilation fans.

By the end of 1908, both shafts had been taken down to a depth of 650 yards where they encountered the Dunsil Seam which the company intended to work at a later date. Headings in the Barnsley Seam were constructed from the pit bottom through the 850 yard diameter shaft pillar in order to open several longwall coal faces to work the coal. The first miners came to work at Bentley from Barber Walker's High Park & Watnall Collieries in Nottinghamshire and by early 1909, 700 men were employed at the colliery as it started to move towards maximum production. Contemporary with the early development of the underground workings was the construction of Bentley New Village to house the first employees.

Bentley Colliery in 1908 published as a postcard by Edgar Scrivens. The massive nature of the wooden framed headgears over No. 1 & 2 shafts can be seen on the left and they are ready to raise coal. Construction of the surface buildings is continuing apace.

By early 1910 a workforce of 1,000 at the pit were producing 2,000 tons of coal per day and it was hoped to triple both these figures within a few years. In recognition of this Barber Walker decided to replace the wooden headgears with more substantial structures and in that year the No 2 headgear was replaced with a reinforced ferro-concrete hempstead surmounted by a steel lattice headgear. The hempstead, a long building used for transporting the coal from the shaft top, was built by the French engineer Mr Mouchel using the patented designs of another French engineer Francois Hennebique and it is believed that their work at Bentley Colliery is one of the first recorded uses of ferro-concrete in this country.

In 1911, the wooden headgear above the No. 1 shaft was replaced with a similar ferro-concrete hempstead but this time the headgear was constructed of the same material as it was required to enclose the flow of air from the colliery underground workings as this was the upcast shaft. The advantage of the use of ferro-concrete was that the absence of exposed timber, brick and steel would reduce maintenance costs. The hempsteads with their arched windows above and arched openings below had elegant classical elevations, giving them the appearance of being built of rendered brick rather than reinforced concrete and they were pleasing to the eye from an architectural point of view.

This postcard view by James Simonton & Sons of Balby can be dated to 1911 when the wooden headgears were replaced. No. 2 headgear of steel construction has been completed whilst the scaffold surrounds the building of No. 1 headgear from ferro-concrete, one of the earliest known uses for this material in the country.

With all the surface plant in position, Bentley Colliery could now start to maximise production and by the middle of 1912 over 20,000 tons of coal were being produced each week, 2,500 men were employed and Bentley New Village had been completed. Coal was wound up the shafts at a speed of 60 miles per hour and was despatched by the Great Northern Railway to home markets and for export. However, Barber Walker still required more employees as they had plans to further increase production, as Bentley had become a notable success for the company. By 1912 Bentley Colliery produced more coal than the rest of the combined output of Barber Walker's 5 other collieries in Nottinghamshire.

However, national events within the mining industry would prove to be very taxing for the company during 1912. The Mines Act (1911) had forbidden the use of wooden headgear for new collieries. Wooden headgears constructed prior to 1911 were allowed to remain in existence although coincidentally Bentley Colliery had replaced their wooden headgears with stronger ferro-concrete structures in the same year. However, a disaster at Cadeby Colliery in July 1912 with the loss of 88 lives so soon after the introduction of the Mines Act (1911) caused the Mines Inspectorate to clamp down on dangerous conditions in collieries in order to prevent another pit disaster like that at Cadeby, and consequently the Mines Inspectorate paid a visit to Bentley Colliery.

It was well known that Bentley would be a troublesome mine as the Barnsley Coal Seam was liable to spontaneous combustion with the emission of enormous quantities of flammable methane which would have to be diluted and rendered harmless by adequate ventilation. Coal was worked by the advancing longwall method and this created problems with spontaneous combustion which caused underground fires in the 'gob' or areas in which the coal had already been mined. Since Bentley Colliery opened in 1908 there had been 40 small underground fires and the colliery was found to contravene several safety aspects of the Mines Act (1911). Thus the Mines Inspectorate, a department of the Government's Home Office, decided to prosecute Barber Walker and made an attempt to close the colliery which they considered was in a highly dangerous condition.

As a result of this Barber Walker & Co., John Fryar, the General Manager and Robert Clive, the Colliery Manager were summoned for prosecution at a hearing on 16th November 1912 and were prosecuted by the Government Home Office who stated that "the colliery was in a highly dangerous condition and that several serious contraventions of the Mines Act (1911) had been committed". Such were the seriousness of the prosecution that it looked likely that Bentley Colliery would have to be closed down. However, Barber Walker was able to launch a successful appeal and the courts overturned the decision of the Home Office. However, this was dependant on the implementation of various safety measures which included an increase in ventilation and enabling each district of the underground workings to be able to be sealed off from the others in case of fire. One outcome from the appeal was the formation of the Doncaster Coal Owner's

Committee, established by John Fryar and the Brodsworth Colliery Chairman Sir Arthur Markham. The Committee opened a laboratory at Bentley Colliery where they published the results of original research into spontaneous combustion and rescue apparatus. This ultimately led to the opening of the Doncaster Mines Rescue Station on Wheatley Hall Road in Doncaster.

From 1913, once the necessary safety measures had been put into place at the pit, Bentley Colliery entered a period of solid achievement. In 1914 a second rail outlet was opened to the west when a connection was made with the Hull & Barnsley & Great Central Railway's Joint Line which enabled Bentley coal to be exported to the continent and South America from Hull Docks. Despite the onset of the First World War and the loss of some of the staff due to enlistment, Bentley continued to produce vast quantities of coal to help the war effort.

In 1915, John Fryar died at the age of 46 following an appendix operation. The highlight of his mining career had been the sinking of the two shafts of Bentley Colliery through the troublesome quicksand. He was replaced as General Manager of Barber Walker & Co. by Mr Coningsby Phillips, formerly manager of Cadeby Colliery.

Following the end of the First World War, Barber Walker & Co was restructured in 1918 as a limited liability company, Barber Walker & Co. Ltd. with a capital of £1,000,000. 50% of the company was held by Major Thomas Barber and 40% was owned by E. L Walker-Munro representing the descendants of the Walker family. The remaining 10% of the shares were in the ownership of various shareholders. The company were looking to repeat the success of Bentley Colliery and used their war time profits that the pit had generated to open another large colliery to the south of Doncaster at Harworth near Bawtry.

One of the first acts of the new company was the opening of a large 'Baum' washing and screening plant at Bentley Colliery in 1918, erected by Simon Carves Ltd., and this replaced the older Luhrig washery. Waste material generated from the screens and washery was tipped onto the fields to the north of the pit. Over the years this tip would grow to be one of the largest in the country, not in height, but in volume and area covered.

In the meantime Bentley Colliery continued to go from strength to strength throughout the 1920s, and between 1912 and 1930 the pit had managed to produce an average of over 1,000,000 tons of coal per year, production figures that became the envy of other colliery owners in the country. Bentley achieved

Two postcard views of Bentley Colliery by Edgar Scrivens c1914 showing the reconstructed surface buildings. **Above:** No 2 headgear positioned above the ferro-concrete hempstead structure which straddled the railway sidings. **Below:** The colliery as viewed from the top end of The Avenue with 8 of the 10 officials' houses which opened in 1907 on the left. No 1 & 2 headgears and corresponding winding engine houses and pit chimney are on the left, colliery offices and coal washery on the right. The Colliery is now about to enter an era of sustained production averaging around 1,000,000 tons of coal per year for the next 15 years.

its record daily output of 5,546 tons on 5th December 1927. Record weekly output of 28,100 tons occurred in May 1922 and the highest monthly output of 108,999 tons was obtained in July 1924. The pit's highest annual output of 1,205,609 tons was achieved in 1924. In 1928 over 4,000 men were employed at the pit, the highest number ever on the payroll.

Throughout the 1920s, Bentley Colliery was very profitable for Barber Walker who, perhaps due to their success with the colliery, donated £5,000 towards the building of Doncaster Royal Infirmary. In 1922 Bentley was the first pit in the Doncaster area to install underground trains to transport the men from the pit bottom to the coal faces and in 1925 they announced that they would be the first Doncaster pit to work the Dunsil Coal Seam located 20 yards beneath the Barnsley Seam. In February 1926, a visit of the Midland Institute of Mining Engineers said that "Bentley Colliery is the best laid out pit in the country".

However, things changed drastically for the worse on Friday 20th November 1931 when a serious underground explosion occurred at Bentley Colliery at around 6:30pm. The explosion occurred in the North East district of the Barnsley Seam instantly killing 43 miners and injuring 4 others, 2 of whom were to later die from their injuries. The cause of the explosion was thought to be a defective safety lamp.

Later that evening crowds of people had gathered outside the pit waiting for news of survivors and by 8pm the Mines Rescue Team had descended the pit with breathing apparatus and equipment. They found 18 miners trapped by the accompanying roof fall from the explosion, including Frank Sykes, Norman McMullen and John Ward who had courageously assisted with the rescuing of the injured men before the official rescue party arrived. By 11pm Major Barber the Chairman and Mr Phillips the General Manager had arrived by motor car from Eastwood Hall and they were joined by various union officials including the president Herbert Smith and secretary Joseph Jones and the Government's Mines Inspectorate. By 2am the following day the district had been made safe and the terrible task of recovering the dead bodies had commenced. King George V contributed the following message: "The Queen and I are shocked to hear of the disaster which occurred last night at Bentley Colliery and send our heartfelt sympathy to the families of those who have lost lives so tragically. I trust that you will be able to give reassuring news of the men who are injured".

On Wednesday 25th November 1931 a crowd of 3,000 people attended the funeral of 31 of the 45 victims. The procession made its way from Bentley Colliery to Arksey Cemetery where the bodies were buried in a communal grave.

Unfortunately 5 bodies were never able to be recovered as they were buried in a sealed off area of the mine.

The Mayor of Doncaster immediately started a relief fund as there were estimated to be 150 dependants. The fund closed on reaching £40,000 and included donations of £2,000 from Barber Walker, £2,000 from the Yorkshire Miners Association, £1,000 from the people of Halifax, £150 from the King and Queen and £1,984 collected in over 400 Co-operative branches.

On Sunday 20th November 1932 a memorial to the 45 Bentley disaster victims was unveiled at Arksey Cemetery comprising a stone obelisk standing in the centre of the communal grave. Twelve of the people involved in rescuing the wounded were awarded certificates and cheques from the Carnegie Hero Fund Trustees and 6 of these received the Edward Medal from King George at a ceremony at Buckingham Palace. Every year a service is held in Arksey Cemetery to remember all those who died at Bentley Colliery.

A poignant scene recorded as a postcard by an anonymous photographer and captioned 'Burial of the victims of the Bentley Colliery Disaster Nov 20th 1931'. The large communal grave in Arksey Cemetery is clearly shown laid out with 21 coffins.

Following the disaster Bentley Colliery intended to return to full production but the economic depression of the early 1930s saw the implementation of a quota

17

system imposed throughout the coal industry to stem over production which would have led to a collapse in the price of coal. Like many collieries, Bentley was allocated a quota equivalent to 66% of its 1920s annual production and due to the reduced output many miners were laid off by the pit at this time although many were taken on in the later 1930s as the economic climate improved.

Another problem for Bentley Colliery in the 1930s was that of flooding. The earliest effects of coal subsidence had been recognised in the area back in 1912 and the area around Bentley was mostly below the 25 feet contour and by the early 1930s this area had sunk by 4 feet due to the effects of coal subsidence. To compound matters, a linear shaped pillar of coal 10,000,000 tons in weight had been left under the River Don to protect the river. This had the effect at keeping the river at its original height whilst the surrounding flood plains had been reduced to a lower level by subsidence. Consequently when the River Don burst its banks the flood water stayed on the low lying flood plains for weeks on end, a feature that would be dramatically repeated in the flooding of Bentley and Toll Bar in the summer of 2007.

Bentley Colliery during the floods of 1932 as featured on a postcard by Arjay Productions of Doncaster. The floods caused the pit to remain idle for 2 weeks. However, due to the effects of subsidence, the flood waters took several weeks to recede and the colliery returned to work as evidenced by the smoke emanating from the pit chimney. The colliery spoil heap is beginning to accumulate on the left and would eventually grow to cover a large surface area.

In September 1931, May 1932, March 1933 and February 1941 major floods occurred in the Bentley and Arksey areas caused by heavy rainfall and melting snow from the Pennines. The flood of May 1932 was the worst when 4,100 acres were under water which stood 10 feet deep in some of the streets of Bentley. This caused the pit to stop work for 2 weeks whilst engineers managed to complete work to stop water pouring down the shafts and thus flooding the underground workings. The flood water remained in the area for several weeks and 953 families vacated their homes, but many others remained in the upstairs of their homes, going for supplies in boats and in fact due to the longevity of the floods, temporary boat landing stages and wooden walkways were constructed along several of the streets in the district.

It was obvious that after 3 consecutive years of floods, something had to be done and the Don Drainage Commissioners, Bentley Urban District Council and Bentley and Bullcroft Collieries met to implement plans to improve drainage. However, due to continual arguments over who was to pay for the scheme, it wasn't until 1939 after the petitioning of the Government, that plans were put into operation. These included the construction of drainage dykes, pumping stations and flood embankments and this work was completed by 1942 although floods would return to the area in 1947 and 2007.

Through the rest of the 1930s, the improving economic situation saw production at Bentley Colliery increase year by year until in 1939 an annual output of over 1,000,000 tons of coal was achieved for the first time since 1930. Pithead baths opened in 1935 at a cost of £30,000 erected by the Miners Welfare Committee. This organisation had been formed following the Mining Industry Act (1920) for purposes connected with the social well-being, recreation and conditions of those who worked in the industry. It was funded by a levy of one penny on every ton of coal produced and from its funds it contributed to the building of numerous Miners Welfare buildings and pithead bath schemes which could then be used by the workforce for a small weekly deduction from their wages. The pithead baths at Bentley Colliery were by the architect C. G. Kemp and were built to a distinctive art deco style with the use of brick and glass blocks. They were opened by the Miners President Herbert Smith and Mr Smithson of the Miners Welfare Committee.

By 1937, there were only 26,000,000 tons of coal left in the Barnsley Seam within Bentley Colliery's royalty and it was announced that in order to ensure the long term survival of the pit, the Company would deepen the shafts to enable production from the Parkgate Seam which would eventually be fully developed to replace the expected falling output from the Barnsley Seam. It was estimated that there were 59,000,000 tons of coal reserves in the Parkgate Seam which was already being worked by the nearby Brodsworth Colliery.

On 12th December 1937 work started on deepening the No. 1 shaft and this work was carried out on the night shifts when coal winding did not take place. This work was completed on October 28th 1938 when the 5 feet thick Parkgate Seam was encountered at a depth of 830 yards and the shaft was continued downwards to a depth of 862 yards in order to tap the Thorncliffe Seam which had a thickness of 4 feet 8 inches. The deepening of the No. 1 shaft was completed on 11th March 1939 when Barber Walker announced plans to take on more workers to develop these seams.

However, the declaration of the Second World War caused these plans to be postponed as the equipment and workforce were not readily available to deepen the No. 2 shaft. Once again many miners enlisted as soldiers despite the fact that mining was a protected occupation and their loss in numbers was partially supplemented by the use of Bevan Boys. In 1942 a second seam was worked at the pit, not the Parkgate as had been intended, but the Dunsil Seam which was only 20 yards beneath the Barnsley Seam and was easily accessed by the tunnelling of drifts from the Barnsley Seam workings. The development of the Dunsil Seam saw the introduction of mechanisation at the coal faces and the transport of the coal from the face to the shafts by underground railways. This mechanism was quickly deployed in the Barnsley Seam workings.

On the 9th February 1944, Bentley Colliery received its first royal visit when a party including King George VI and Queen Elizabeth inspected the pithead baths, screens and surface buildings in the company of Major Barber. It was reported that the royal cars were cheered by crowds of women and children as they drove through the streets of Bentley on the journey back to Doncaster Station.

Following the end of the Second World War the collieries were nationalised and the National Coal Board (N.C.B.) took over the ownership of Bentley Colliery. Barber Walker & Co. Ltd. were paid £1,473,800 for Bentley and Harworth Collieries and the company was finally wound up on the 27th April 1954 and Major Thomas Barber, the chairman, retired having been in the position since 1897. Coningsby Philips, the general manger since 1915, joined the N.C.B. upon nationalisation. Throughout the 1950s the workforce at Bentley Colliery averaged 2,800 who continued to produce around 1,000,000 tons of coal per year from the Barnsley and Dunsil Seams.

In 1958 the pit celebrated its 50th year of operation and the Bentley Miners Welfare and N.C.B. organised a programme of golden jubilee celebrations. By 1958, Bentley Colliery had produced around 50,000,000 tons of coal, an average of 1,000,000, tons per year which is an incredible achievement from a single colliery over such a long time span.

In the 1960s, the N.C.B. introduced further improvements at Bentley Colliery. These included the opening of a new coal preparation plant and rapid loading bunker to supply trains of coal for electricity generation. Modernisation of the pit bottom saw the use of skip winding facilities introduced at the shafts. The old brick built steam powered winding engine houses were replaced with new buildings containing electrically driven winding engines and the demolition of one of the unique ferro-concrete hempsteads took place. The increasing use of mechanisation and the removal of coal by the more economical retreat mining method saw the employment figure fall to around 2,200. This fall was also matched by a significant drop in output due to dwindling reserves in the Barnsley and Dunsil Seams

Because of this the 1970s saw the exploitation of other coal seams including the Swallow Wood Seam to replace the falling output from the Barnsley and Dunsil Seams. In the 1980s it was finally decided to mine the Parkgate Seam, a project which had been commenced in the 1930s when the No. 1 shaft was deepened to this seam but from which no coal had been extracted as the project was abandoned due to the outbreak of the Second World War. The No. 2 shaft was deepened to 830 yards and the first Parkgate Seam coal was produced in 1987. This had the effect of increasing output and Bentley once again was producing 1,000,000 tons per year.

However, in the early 1990s there was a reduced demand for British Coal in a highly competitive market place following the development of several Gas-fired power stations and on the 23rd November 1993 British Coal announced the proposed closure of Bentley Colliery. By the end of 1993 production had ceased and during 1994 the site was wound down and the final coal was despatched by train from Bentley Colliery. Subsequently the buildings were demolished in late 1994 and early 1995. As a memorial to all those who worked at the colliery one of the pit wheels was placed alongside the cricket ground in The Avenue.

During the summer of 1998 work commenced on a £8,360,000 scheme to restore the 247 acres site into a country park and community forest and these plans included the building of wetlands and a nature reserve. In the early years of the 21st Century the new national recreational trail known as the Trans Pennine Trail was routed across the site and today the area forms part of Bentley Community Forest.

Above: Bentley Colliery in 1992, featuring the electric winding engine houses which date from the reconstruction of the 1970s. *Below:* Bentley Colliery undergoing demolition in 1994 leaving the pioneering ferro-concrete hempstead structure standing, possibly due to an unsuccessful attempt to have the building listed by English Heritage as this structure was finally demolished in 1995. (Photographers unknown, Stan Longley Collection)

Bentley New Village

In 1901 the population of the parish of Bentley with Arksey was 2,403 but this was about to undergo a tremendous increase with the development of Bentley Colliery. At this time Arksey was the older settlement dating back to medieval times and Bentley was largely an agricultural settlement with several stone built cottages, a couple of farms, and a Post Office. The old village of Bentley was amply provided with three public houses; the Druid's Arms, Railway Tavern and Bay Horse. However, the construction of a handful of brick built terraces in the late Victorian period saw Bentley begin to develop as a suburb of Doncaster and on 27th October 1903 an electric tramway opened connecting Bentley High Street with the nearby town.

In the first decade of the 20th Century the local authority was Bentley with Arksey Parish Council who together with the West Riding County Council was responsible for the provision of public services in the district. However, the building of local authority houses at this time was largely unheard of and house building was largely in the hands of private or speculative builders who would construct a row of terraces and rent the houses out to tenants, and this would often prove to be a profitable enterprise. With the opening of Bentley Colliery the demand for housing went through the roof and this was met by a combination of private landlord, council and company housing.

The benefits of providing Company owned housing were well known to the colliery owners of the day. Once the expense of constructing the houses had been met, the company could then rent them to their workers who were then tied to working at the colliery and therefore less likely to leave their employment, a particularly important factor when several new collieries in the area were crying out for workers. Another advantage of providing company owned houses was that rent could be deducted from the workers' pay therefore there would be no defaults in payment and should the men go on strike the threat of eviction was a powerful tool which had been used nearby in 1902 and 1905 at Denaby and Hemsworth Collieries respectively when striking miners were turned out of their company owned houses to be replaced by non-striking workers.

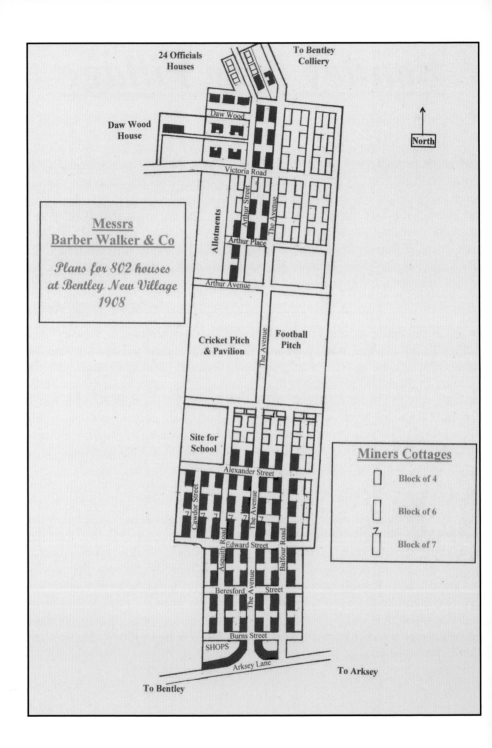

24 Officials Houses

To Bentley Colliery

Daw Wood House

Daw Wood

Victoria Road

North

Messrs Barber Walker & Co

Plans for 802 houses at Bentley New Village 1908

Allotments

Arthur Street

Arthur Place

The Avenue

Arthur Avenue

Cricket Pitch & Pavilion

The Avenue

Football Pitch

Site for School

Alexander Street

Miners Cottages

Block of 4

Block of 6

7 Block of 7

Cawdor Street

Asquith Road

The Avenue

7 7 7 7 7

Edward Street

Balfour Road

Beresford Street

The Avenue

Burns Street

SHOPS

Arksey Lane

To Arksey

To Bentley

24

It was probably due to all of the above reasons that Barber Walker decided to provide its own houses for its workforce. A new road had been built from Arksey Lane to the pit site. This new road, nearly a mile long, was named The Avenue and it was decided to construct a settlement known as New Bentley, or Bentley New Village as it later became known, along either side of The Avenue. Consequently in 1908, Barber Walker commissioned the Doncaster architect, Philip Brundell, who drew up plans for an estate of 802 houses, consisting of 776 miners' cottages, 24 villas for pit officials, and 2 large detached houses for the manager and the agent. To facilitate this it was decided to purchase the freehold of the site from Sir William Cooke and 75 acres were allocated as the site for the New Village which also included the provision of schools, playing grounds, allotments, cricket pitch, football pitch and an undeveloped site which was intended for a Miners Institute. The site would be laid out with two areas of housing with the community buildings in the centre. An area of land was set aside for shops at the entrance to the estate although no allocation was made for a public house.

The first houses built in Bentley New Village were 10 properties at the top of The Avenue to house pit officials, adjacent to the colliery, and these had been completed in 1907 prior to the drawing up of Philip Brundell's plans. In 1909, construction commenced on the first phase of the general housing for Bentley New Village. Blocks of houses, or cottages as they referred to at the time, were built along the northern part of The Avenue and Arthur Street, Arthur Place and Arthur Avenue were laid out.

The cottages were constructed in identical blocks of 6 to two different external designs which were internally identical. In each block the centre 4 houses were built in a similar fashion to a traditional terrace but the houses at the ends of each block were set sideways and they projected forwards from the building line with a large gable to the front and rear which helped to relieve the monotony of the rows of houses. They were brick built with the upper storeys rendered with detailing on the gables and the ridge tiles. The bricks were provided from Barber Walker's Watnall Brickworks in Nottinghamshire. The houses were set back from the street with small front gardens and were provided with rear yards which opened onto a service lane between the rears of the blocks.

Internally, the middle 4 houses were provided with a scullery, living room and downstairs bath and WC whilst upstairs there were 3 bedrooms. The gabled end houses were larger and had an additional parlour downstairs and 3 larger bedrooms upstairs. Presumably this was reflected in a higher rental for the end properties.

In 1910, work started on the second phase of Bentley New Village, this time located around the southern part of The Avenue. This was a much larger area of housing and consisted of Alexander Street, Asquith Road, Balfour Street, Beresford Street, Burns Street, Cawdor Street, and Edward Street. Some of the streets were named after prominent politicians of the day, including prime ministers Herbert Asquith & Arthur Balfour plus cabinet ministers Charles Beresford & the Earl of Cawdor. Again the houses were built in blocks of 6 to two separate external designs with an identical layout to those built in the previous year. However, a slight kink in the alignment of The Avenue caused the construction of a few blocks containing 7 houses with the central house having a gable to the front and rear in a similar fashion to the end houses. By 1911, 414 houses for miners had been completed in Bentley New Village.

The main entrance to Bentley New Village was made from Arksey Lane where a curving parade of shops was positioned at either side of the junction of Arksey Lane and The Avenue. These properties were completed in 1911 and one set was partially occupied by The Doncaster Mutual & Co-operative Society whilst the other set opened as a branch of the famous Doncaster Grocers Hodgson & Hepworths. Other shops in this parade included a pawnbroker which presumably received good custom in the early days.

The last project came in 1912 and saw the construction of 14 villas out of the planned 24 villas intended for colliery officials along Victoria Road and Daw Lane. These provided more extensive accommodation than the standard company housing and they included 4 bedrooms and an upstairs bathroom. The final house to be built was Daw Wood House. This was an extensive property with 18 rooms downstairs and 13 rooms upstairs together with stables and a carriage house. Daw Wood House opened in 1913 and was intended to be the home of the colliery manager but in the end Mr Donald McGregor, the agent to Barber Walker & Co. took up residence. Daw Wood House was set in extensive grounds and surrounded by a seven foot high wall, presumably to give Mr McGregor some privacy from the prying eyes of his new neighbours! Another

Two illustrations featuring The Avenue in Bentley New Village published as postcards by Edgar Scrivens. Both views date from 1913 or 1914 following the extension of the Doncaster Corporation trams from Bentley High Street. Originally it was intended to extend the trams the full length of The Avenue to the colliery gates; however a terminus was made near the junction with Alexander Street and why this was remains unknown, despite the fact that the Bentley route was the most profitable route on the Doncaster tramway network. The designs of Philip Brundell's blocks of 6 houses can be clearly seen. In spite of its name, The Avenue was never planted with trees until relatively recently.

house for the colliery manager, Mr Clive, was built away from the New Village on a site at the junction of Askern Road and Daw Lane.

Although not built along the picturesque lines of nearby Woodlands Model Village, built for nearby Brodsworth Colliery, the housing of Bentley New Village was built to a similar overall plan, i.e. two areas of housing separated by an area of community buildings. However, the key difference to Woodlands is that at Bentley New Village the blocks of houses were laid out to a traditional grid pattern, although there were some attempts to break up the formality with gables and small gardens and the provision of inside toilets. Nevertheless the village was still ahead of its time compared with other areas of contemporary industrial housing. The use of brick and rendering and the detailing to the gables gave a fresh look to the design of the housing. Although Barber Walker referred to their settlement as a Model Village it quickly became known as Bentley New Village. In 1911, Barber Walker appeared happy to relinquish control of the services to the properties and ownership of the roads to the newly formed Bentley Urban District Council.

This postcard from c1913/4 is captioned Model Village Bentley, the name that Barber Walker initially referred to its new settlement as. This view shows the entrance to The Avenue from Arksey Lane with the curving parade of shops on either side, including a branch of the Doncaster grocers Hodgson & Hepworths. Note the children outside Fred Pickersgill's newsagent and sweet shop. Postcard published by Doncaster Rotophoto from a negative by James Simonton & Sons.

An area between the two main areas of housing had been set aside for community use and included a site for schools, an institute, cricket ground, football ground, bowling greens and tennis courts. On the 2nd January 1913 the West Riding County Council opened the New Village Schools at a cost of £10,000; previously the children of the New Village had attended Cooke Street School in Bentley. The Company opened a wooden building as a colliery institute in 1915 which supervised the recreational activities of the area. The building contained assembly rooms, meeting rooms and reading rooms and was initially provided as a temperance institute. This was later replaced by the Miners Welfare building in 1921.

No provision was made in this central community area for religious needs as the new settlement was only a short walk away from the old village of Bentley where Cooke Street Primitive Methodist Chapel, High Street Wesleyan Chapel and St Peters Church had opened in 1857, 1899 & 1898 respectively. Despite this, Bentley New Village would eventually receive its own place of worship through the efforts of the South Yorkshire Coalfield Churches Extension Committee who were looking to serve the spiritual needs of the new colliery districts by the construction of churches paid for entirely by donations. Barber Walker & Co donated a plot of land for the construction of a church on a site on Victoria Road and they donated £1,000 towards its construction as well as agreeing to pay the salary of the new curate. St Philips & St James Church at Bentley New Village was dedicated on 1st May 1915 and this day also saw the opening of the church hall on the opposite side of the road. The church was built to a standard design and is identical to other South Yorkshire Coalfield Churches Extension Committee buildings at Maltby, New Edlington and New Rossington.

The opening of the New Village church in 1915 saw the completion of the company village of New Bentley. Apart from the construction of the villas for officials and Daw Wood House, Barber Walker hadn't built any more houses for their workforce since 1911. The initial plans had shown 776 miners houses of which only 414 had been completed and areas of the New Village were left undeveloped until the 1920s. The architect's plans also show groups of houses in blocks of 4 although none of these were built, presumably because it was cheaper per house to build the larger blocks of 6 & 7. Why Barber Walker failed to complete Philip Brundell's housing plans seems strange when they were crying out for workers in order to increase production. In comparison, by 1912, Brodsworth Colliery owned 964 houses in their villages at Woodlands and Highfields which had cost them £208,000 to build. However, Brodsworth Colliery had a relatively trouble free development and it is likely that at Bentley the unexpected costs incurred due to the delay and difficulties in sinking the shafts restricted the finance for the number of houses that Barber Walker could afford to build. No further Company housing was constructed at Bentley after the First World War and the housing requirements were left to private enterprise and the local authority.

Despite ceasing to build their own accommodation, Bentley Colliery was still trying to increase its workforce in order to increase production and people were attracted to the area to work at the pit as the wages were relatively higher than those many people earned as agricultural labourers or in other trades. All this led to immense pressure for houses which was partially met by speculative builders. At the time Bentley with Arksey Parish Council lacked the resources to build their own houses, which was one of the reasons why they applied for powers to become an Urban District Council in 1911 but even then they were limited in what they could provide until the passing of the Town Planning Act in 1919.

Consequently in the period 1911-1914, just before the First World War, private builders constructed numerous traditional style terraced houses either side of Askern Road, in Bentley West End, Toll Bar and around the old Bentley village, the standard of which varied from poor to good, depending on the builder. The demand for houses was such that it had become a seller's market. The papers of the time reported that miners desperate for a house were paying £5 for the key even before the foundations had been laid and were depositing a week's rent in order to secure a newly built house. In 1901 there were 548 houses in the parish of Bentley with Arksey. This figure had increased to 2,435 by 1915 which housed a population of 13,000. However, there was still a tremendous demand for houses as Barber Walker wished to employ 4,000 men at Bentley Colliery and people were flocking to the pit from all over the country as mining was a relatively well paid and secure employment at the time. The demand for housing led to severe cases of overcrowding as several families shared some of the terraced houses. This in turn led to poor medical conditions and high levels of infant mortality and in 1913 the annual report of the Bentley Urban District Council Medical Officer, Dr Dunne, stated that "overcrowding undoubtedly exists. Everywhere the same tale is told: people can not get houses and some tenants are living in houses before they have been completed".

In 1912 a plan for 477 houses at Toll Bar was unveiled. This settlement was named after the old toll house that stood by the Askern Road although the Toll Bar housing scheme failed to attract enough investors as inflation at the time was rapidly increasing as it now cost £250 to build a standard terraced house. However, around 400 houses were built in the Toll Bar area, but unfortunately to a very poor standard and this has been proved by the demolition of much of the housing in Toll Bar in the 1970s. The original houses of Toll Bar were served by the opening of a Post Office, a general provisions store and a branch of the Doncaster Mutual Co-operative Society.

This postcard is captioned Owston Road, Toll Bar, but actually shows Askern Road running through this settlement of 400 speculatively built terraced houses consisting of Coney Road, Manor Road, Grange Road and Prospect Roads, plus housing near the Brickyards on Adwick Lane. Toll Bar is named after an old toll house built to serve the Doncaster & York turnpike road and the toll house was later converted into a club. J M Cooper's grocers and off licence shown on the right was the only shop until the opening of the post office and a branch of The Doncaster Mutual Co-operative Society in 1913. Postcard published by Doncaster Rotophoto c1914.

An interesting school strike occurred in Toll Bar in 1913 when many of the parents of Toll Bar stopped their children from attending schools in Bentley due to the state of the muddy roads in the district. This may seem trivial today but it must be remembered that the roads were in a dire state at the time due to all the building work, sewer construction and the building of the railway line that separated Toll Bar from Bentley and the objection was primarily over the children having to spend all day at school in wet and muddy clothes. The school strike obviously had the desired effect as the West Riding County Council provided Toll Bar with temporary schools which were replaced with permanent school buildings in 1914.

The years just before the First World War saw significant changes to the old village of Bentley. Properties on the south side of the High Street were largely demolished and rebuilt to facilitate road widening and numerous shops opened to serve the needs of the new settlements, including a third branch of the Doncaster Mutual Co-operative Society in the Bentley area which opened in 1913, only to be replaced with larger premises next door in 1921. In 1914 on a site adjacent to the Co-operative, the Bentley Coliseum Cinema opened which proved to be a very popular entertainment establishment. In 1913 the Doncaster Corporation trams were finally extended to from the High Street in old Bentley village along Arksey Lane to Bentley New Village where they terminated in The Avenue. The West End area was provided with a large public house on Watch House Lane, the Bentley Drum Hotel, and the West Riding County Council opened Kirkby Avenue Schools in 1911 which relieved the overcrowding in the Cooke Street schools in Bentley old village.

Following the granting of urban powers in 1911, the first project that Bentley Urban District Council instigated was the provision of a comprehensive sewage system. Once this had been completed in 1913, they looked at providing their own houses to help alleviate the housing shortage. In 1914 they paid Barber Walker £1,500 for 6 acres of land between Askern Road and Daw Lane adjacent to the pit manager's house. The newly formed Urban District Council was quite dynamic for the time and it laid out a development of 99 houses, some of the first council houses built in the country. These were built in blocks of 3, 4 & 6 and comprised Fisher Street and French Street with a frontage to Askern Road. These houses were built to a good standard and received favourable comments from the local press. However, once the first families had moved in it was reported that there were still nearly 300 families waiting for houses in the Bentley area.

The outbreak of the First World War saw the cessation of any further house building in the area and it was not until the Government of the day passed the Town Planning Act (1919) that grants and loans were awarded to local councils to provide their own authority owned housing. By this time it was reported that 800 families were now waiting for houses in Bentley and in the early 1920s Bentley Urban District Council embarked on a major house building scheme which was to turn out to be significant achievement from such a small local authority.

Housing constructed by Bentley Urban District Council is featured in these coloured postcards from the 1930s published by R.A.P. Co. of London. **Above:** *Askern Road with the development of 99 houses on the right in 1914, some of the earliest council built houses in the country.* **Below:** *Victoria Road featuring some of the 674 houses built by the authority in the early 1920s making a total of 773 houses owned by the Bentley Urban District Council, a significant achievement for such a small council. Note the trolleybus wires which replaced the Bentley tramways in 1931. Plans to extend the trolleybuses to Toll Bar were never implemented.*

A large area of land between Bentley New Village and Askern Road was earmarked for the development of a council estate and building commenced in 1922 with the construction of 514 houses all in the form of semi detached 3 bedroom properties with gardens to the front and rear. They differed from their pre First World War cousins in being provided with an upstairs bathroom. This estate included the laying out of Winnipeg Road, Rosslyn Crescent, Hawthorne Grove, Daw Lane and Victoria Road. Several areas in Bentley New Village which had lain undeveloped since 1911 were purchased from Barber Walker and houses were built on Elm Crescent and parts of The Avenue. 86 additional houses were built near the centre of Bentley and an estate of 74 houses was provided in Arksey. By 1924, Bentley Urban District Council had constructed 674 semi-detached houses, all built and occupied within three years, a significant building achievement for such a small authority which helped to substantially reduce the demand for houses. Additional housing was provided by speculative builders, although on a smaller scale than that provided before the First World War. One significant development was the building of 96 houses in The Homestead adjacent to Arksey Lane. A site at the corner of Askern Road and Victoria Road was sold to Johns Smiths brewery who built a large public house, the Magnet Hotel.

Further developments in the 1920s included the opening of a Roman Catholic Church on High Street and Roman Catholic Schools near Arksey Lane. A Secondary Modern School was opened next to Bentley St Peter's Church and a Baptist Church opened on Askern Road. At the junction of Askern Road and Winnipeg Road a large memorial to the work of the St John's Ambulance Brigade was unveiled.

Other developments in the 1920s saw the opening in 1921 of the New Village Colliery Institute on one of the undeveloped sites on The Avenue. This building included a large hall seating 400, bars, games and billiards rooms and facilities for the adjacent cricket and football pitches. The running of this facility passed from Barber Walker to the Miners Welfare Scheme in 1923. Additional recreational facilities were provided jointly by the Miners Welfare Scheme and Bentley Urban District Council when 18 acres of land near Askern Road and Cooke Street were converted into a public park, featuring pleasure grounds, bandstands, a sand pit and play area, bowling greens and 4 tennis courts, together with a large Miners Welfare Pavilion. These amenities formed part of Bentley Park and they were opened on Saturday 15th September 1923 by Mr Roberts, the chairman of Bentley Urban District Council, and Mr Shinwell, the Government Minster for Mines. Bentley Park was very well received by the residents of Bentley and proved especially popular in the inter-war years.

In 1924, Sir William Cooke, no doubt enriched with the proceeds from the coal royalties, disposed of his Wheatley Hall estate and retired to his estate in Oxfordshire where he lived until his death in 1964. Barber Walker purchased 1,000 acres of the estate which they farmed themselves adding them to the farms in Scawthorpe that they had purchased back in 1904. A Farm Manager was appointed to oversee the farming side and he lived at Scawthorpe Grange whilst Mr McGregor moved from Daw Wood House to take up residence at Scawthorpe Hall.

31.26. The Sand Pit. M.W. Park. Bentley. J.S.&S.

This charming scene depicts a crowded sand pit in Bentley Park which opened in 1923. Municipal parks were extremely well used during the interwar years and Bentley Park, with its swings, tennis courts and bowling greens, was no exception as evidenced by this view dating from 1932 and published as a postcard by James Simonton & Sons.

The Bentley area had undergone a developmental boom in the period 1908-1914 and again from 1920-1925 due to the tremendous demand for housing to provide for the workforce at Bentley Colliery which produced 1,000,000 tons of coal per year throughout the 1920s. However the economic boom of the time was coming to an end and the Roaring Twenties were followed by the depression of the 1930s and the pit was imposed with the quota system to limit output in order to protect the national price of coal from collapse. Consequently little development took place in Bentley in the 1930s although one change that occurred in 1931 was the replacement of the trams with a trolleybus service which was extended in a loop from the old tram terminus in The Avenue, via Victoria Road and Askern Road back to Bentley High Street.

Following the Second World War further areas of council housing were built on Barber Walker's farmland in the Scawthorpe area together with 300 houses provided by the National Coal Board which largely housed miners from Newcastle and Scotland who transferred to South Yorkshire following the closure of their own collieries in the 1960s.

Bentley Colliery continued to produce significant quantities of coal under N.C.B. ownership until its closure in 1993 brought economic hardship to the area. Since then Bentley has looked towards Doncaster for most of its employment and has more or less become a suburb of the town.

This Memorial to Bentley Colliery, formed from two coal cutting drums, has been positioned on top of the spoil heap overlooking the site of Bentley Colliery, which has now been landscaped to form a country park, Bentley Community Woodland. In the distance can be seen 8 of the 10 officials houses constructed at the top of The Avenue in 1907 prior to the drawing up of the plans for Bentley New Village.

Glossary

Barnsley Coal Seam
A seam of coal up to 10 feet thick within the Coal Measures of South Yorkshire which is only found at the surface near the town of Barnsley.

Bunker
A large container used for the storage of coal before the coal can be treated in the screens and washery of a coal preparation plant.

Cage
Steel structure used to transport men or coal filled tubs up and down the shafts. Some cages had two decks. The cage was attached by a steel rope to the winding engine.

Coal Measures
A thick sequence of rocks and strata which consists of sandstones, shales, clays and coal seams. The coal measures of Yorkshire contain around 30 different coal seams.

Coal Preparation Plant.
A building where the treatment of coal is undertaken prior to dispatch, usually containing screens, washery and a conveyor leading to a rapid loading bunker.

Coalfield (Exposed & Concealed)
An area of land above coal measure rocks. A coalfield may be "exposed", i.e. the coal measures are found at the surface, or "concealed" where they are hidden at greater depths beneath younger rocks. Doncaster is situated on a concealed coalfield where the coal measures are buried beneath Magnesian Limestone and Bunter Sandstones.

Drift
A sloping tunnel connecting coal seams to the base of the shafts or to the surface.

Fault
A geological fracture resulting from the upward or downward movement of the strata on either side.

Gob

The area left following removal of a coal seam. It is supported with waste material or allowed to collapse in a controlled way.

Headgear

A structure of wooden, steel lattice or reinforced concrete construction situated above the shafts and used to support the winding wheel.

Longwall Mining

A method of coal working in which coal is mined from a long coal face. The coal face connects two tunnels which lead back to the base of the shafts. The coalface thus advances away from the shafts leaving an area of gob behind. This method was later replaced by retreat mining.

Main

A suffix used mainly in South Yorkshire to denote those collieries which mined the largest or main seam from the coal measures, i.e. the Barnsley Seam

Pillar and Stall Mining

A method of coal working where coal was extracted from areas known as stalls leaving pillars of coal to support the surface. Largely replaced with longwall mining due to the advance in technology in the 19th Century.

Pit

A local term for a coal mine or colliery

Rapid Loading Bunker

A large bunker containing many tons of coal which is dropped into railway wagons passing beneath the structure.

Retreat Mining

The most economical method in mining in which roadways are driven out to the extremity of the royalty to where a coal face can then be worked back towards the shaft bottom. Largely superseded longwall mining in the 1950s/1960s.

Roadways

Underground tunnels leading from the bottom of the shaft to the coal faces.

Royalty

An area of land beneath which coal can be extracted by paying a fee or royalty on every ton produced to the landowner.

Screens
A building containing numerous devices for sorting individual lumps of coal by size or weight

Shafts
A vertical tunnel from the surface to the coal seam through which the coal is extracted and men and materials can access the workings. Following a mining disaster at Hartley Colliery in County Durham each colliery was required to have two shafts, downcast and upcast, to aid escape in the event of an accident. Air was pumped through the downcast shaft to ventilate the workings and then drawn out of the colliery via the upcast shaft.

Shaft Pillar
An area of coal left intact in order to support the colliery's surface buildings and thus protect them from the effects of subsidence. Some coal was removed from the shaft pillar to form roadways or tunnels to access the underground workings.

Sinking
The process of tunnelling vertically downwards from the surface to the coal seam in order to construct a shaft, usually undertaken by workers called sinkers who specialised in this highly skilled but dangerous work.

Skip Winding
A method of winding coal up a shaft by the use of a large capacity metal container or skip. A more economical way of transport than that previously used when individual coal filled tubs were brought to the surface in a cage.

Tubbing
A waterproof casing, usually of iron, inserted into a shaft as it was sunk in order to keep back water and soft sediments.

Tubs
Small wagons used to transport coal underground, usually hauled by pit ponies.

Washery
A surface plant for dealing with the cleaning and washing of coal

Winding Engine
Engine, initially steam driven but later powered by electricity, used to raise the cages up and down the shafts.

Bibliography

Barnett, A L (1984). *The Railways of the South Yorkshire Coalfield from 1880.* RCTS Publishing, Devon.

Colliery Guardian (1927). *The Colliery Year Book & Coal Trades Directory.* Louis Cassier Publishing, London.

Gould S & Ayris I (1995). *Colliery Landscapes. An aerial survey of the deep-mined coal industry in England.* English Heritage / Billington Press Ltd, London.

Hill, Alan (2001). *The South Yorkshire Coalfield, a history and development.* Tempus Publishing, Stroud.

Oakley, Gillian (2002). *Progress in the Parish: Colliery development and Local Government in the Doncaster Coalfield, 1905-1915.* PhD Thesis, The University of Leeds, School of History.

Thornes, Robin (1994). *Images of Industry: Coal.* Royal Commission on the historical monuments of England, Swindon.

Whitelock, G C H. (1955). *250 years in coal. The History of Barber Walker and Company Ltd, 1680-1946.* Published privately by the Company.